Coping when your **parents** separate

Bill Merrington

kevin
mayhew

First published in 2007 by

KEVIN MAYHEW LTD
Buxhall, Stowmarket, Suffolk, IP14 3BW
E-mail: info@kevinmayhewltd.com
Web: www.kevinmayhew.com

Also by Bill Merrington:

Suffering Love – how parents cope with the death of children

Coping with the Sudden Death of a Parent
(previously known as The Hideaway*)*

Coping with the Death of a Parent through Illness
(previously known as Alice's Dad*)*

First Response to Grief and Loss – a manual and DVD for professional workers engaging with children and young people

9 8 7 6 5 4 3 2 1 0

ISBN 978 1 84417 790 5
Catalogue No 1501017

Cover and typeset design by Sara-Jane Came
Typeset by Fiona Connell-Finch
Printed and bound in Great Britain

Contents

For

Tabatha and Skimble
our first cats,
and all the children at
Ilmington Primary School,
Warwickshire,
where I have had
the privilege
of taking assemblies

Introduction

Everyone who gets married starts out with the same intention: to live together happily for the rest of their lives. Many of them go on to have children and live together, despite ups and downs. However, some find that, for one reason or another, life together is just not working. In some situations blame seems to lie squarely at the feet of one partner, but more often than not the reasons are complicated and both must take responsibility for the separation.

Adults, on the whole, are able to take care of themselves, but what about the children who get caught up in it all? *Coping when Your Parents Separate* is the story of a brother and sister's experience of what happens when their parents separate. They find themselves on a journey which is hard to handle. How do they feel about their parents? Do they blame themselves for their parents' separation? How do they cope with the changes that are taking place in their lives?

Coping When Your Parents Separate is aimed at children under 12 in particular, but has been written for anyone, young or old, who is grappling with the consequences when parents split up. For those in a similar situation, the book will enable them to see themselves within the story, and, I hope, find tools to aid their recovery and growth. The story and notes on each chapter provide an opportunity for people to look at their own emotions and feelings.

Teachers and counsellors will find the book a useful aid in encouraging young people to discuss their understanding of separation and divorce. The story will enable young people to reflect upon how they react to their emotions and feelings.

I meet many adults who seek to protect their children from thinking about what might be happening to them within the family. However, I am convinced we must be willing to talk; to share and discuss family issues with our children. I hope *Coping when Your Parents Separate* proves to be a useful tool in aiding this discussion.

Finally, if you find yourself in some way identifying with the children in this story, may I encourage you to share your feelings and experiences with someone you trust. I do not know your story or how you feel, but I do know, from listening to many people, that sharing your experience can help you to find growth points in your life.

If you would like to share your story, and feel you have no one to talk to, then you are welcome to write to me by sending an e-mail to Counselling Bereaved Parents and Children at *support@counsellingcare.org*

BILL MERRINGTON

Coping when your parents separate

The tall flat

Alice and Peter had just returned with their parents from a coach trip to a show in London called *Cats*. The music lingered in Alice's head for days afterwards, while Peter kept repeating all the funny names they had heard for the cats. The twins lived in a flat on the third floor with their Mum and Dad.

It wasn't long before Alice and Peter were pestering their parents for a cat of their own. However, their parents had other things on their minds. Mum and Dad had recently been arguing a lot with each other. Perhaps because of this, their parents gave in to the idea of having a cat. 'We can't just get one cat,' said Peter, 'we must have one each.' At first Mum was determined just to get one cat that was already fully grown, but one night Dad came home with news that a colleague at work had a cat that had just had kittens. 'Please can we go and see?' asked Alice.

Something to think about and do...

Have you been somewhere special that you remember?

Can you draw/paint a special occasion that you remember?

Listen to a special piece of music that you like.

A friend's house

Dad's friend opened the door and welcomed the family in. 'The kittens are in the kitchen at the moment, but we only have two left.' Before he'd finished speaking, the twins had dashed into the kitchen and were kneeling down in joy. 'Look, Mum, aren't they beautiful!' exclaimed Alice. Mum, who was the member of the family least keen on animals, had to admit that the kittens did indeed look lovely. The two kittens were fast asleep with their mother. 'This one's mine,' said Peter. 'He's got a great black and white stripy coat.' 'Well you guessed right,' said Dad's friend, 'it is a he. The other one is his sister.' Alice's eyes opened wide as she reached over to the female kitten. 'She's so colourful, Mum, white, golden brown and black.'

'It would be a shame to split them up,' said Dad, looking at Mum. Now everyone was looking at Mum. All those eyes staring at her, she couldn't help but say yes. 'Only on the condition that you look after them, do you hear me?' she warned.

Something to think about and do…

Do you love animals?
What's your favourite?

What pets do you have or would you like to have one day?

Can you draw or paint them, or perhaps make them in plasticine?

Can you create a new animal that would be special only to you?

A special place

A few days later, when the children had acquired a basket, cat food and a knitted mouse on a string, the kittens arrived. At first they sniffed around the room cautiously, but soon found themselves at home. Each had a special place to curl up and fall asleep in. The female loved to jump into the rocking chair, while her brother preferred to lie right next to the radiator. However, they also had times of great activity. It wasn't long before they were both chasing each other around the flat. 'Careful,' shouted Mum, as they dashed up the curtains onto the bookshelves and down under the settee. 'It's time we named them, I think.' This proved to be more difficult than expected. The twins just couldn't decide on names. 'Mum, how did you decide our names?' Alice asked. 'Well,' said Mum, 'you've got your grandmother's middle name. We struggled to decide on Peter's name, so we looked in a baby naming book.' 'What's that?' enquired Peter. 'It's just what it says it is: a book full of names from A to Z with each name having a description about its history and meaning.'

Something to think about and do...

Where do you feel safe?

Do you have a special friend to share with?

Can you remember a place that was very special for you? (e.g. on holiday, perhaps at the beach or up a mountain)

Have you got a special toy or possession that comforts you?

Try and find a comfortable, safe place where you can close your eyes, relax your body and picture and think about your special place. Use this exercise when you need to relax and escape the pressures of the day.

A to Z of names

Peter's mind was racing. 'What does my name mean?' he asked. Mum went to the bookshelf and found the baby naming book. She sat on the settee, and with the two children sitting either side of her, she found the names that began with the letter P. Mum explained that the name Peter came from the Bible and meant 'rock'. 'Let me have it, Mum, I want to find my name.' But before Mum could pass the book to Alice, Peter had snatched it. At first, Peter felt strange that his name was based on something as simple as a rock. But as he read the book, he soon discovered that to be named after Jesus' disciple was very special. 'The name means you have to be very solid, reliable and helpful,' explained Mum. Peter's chest swelled with pride.

'Why don't you both sit on the settee and see if you can find names for the kittens?' Mum suggested. So for the next hour, Peter and Alice, with both kittens sitting on their laps, had fun looking through the book and laughing at some of the more unusual names. Despite Peter and Alice looking and looking they still couldn't decide on any names. 'I know,' said Alice, 'let's get the programme out from the show we went to see. It might give us some ideas.' In the end they decided that the ginger and white female was to be called Tabatha and the striped male black cat, Skimble.

Something to think about and do...

What names would you choose?

What is your name and do you know its meaning?

Why was it chosen?

Look at your birth certificate. Can you redesign your birth certificate using additional information you can find out from your relatives? What day and time of the week was it? Who visited you? What were your first presents? What other names might you have been called?

Get a large piece of paper (lining or wallpaper works well) and get someone to draw around your body. Inside the body add everything that makes you special, e.g. favourite food, activities, sport, friends, colour of your hair, eyes, etc.

Write your name on the paper. Try writing the name in different ways, e.g. like a barcode.

Write underneath: 'I'm special.'

The whistle

Life with two energetic kittens soon became routine. Mum would feed them and tidy up after one of their frantic chases around the flat. The job she least liked was cleaning the litter tray. It was Peter's job to remember to put out the food twice daily. At first he wanted to fill the cats' bowls to the brim. But Peter soon realised that the cats preferred to eat small amounts and often wouldn't eat what had been put out earlier. Alice's task was simply to pamper them with lots of cuddles and try to persuade them to sit on her lap. Each cat had its own particular characteristics. Skimble was definitely the boss. He would chase Tabatha and pounce on her. He seemed especially to enjoy waking Tabatha up when she was asleep. Skimble was the more mischievous cat, while Tabatha was more placid. But strangely, it was Skimble who would jump up onto the children's laps while Tabatha would only do so when picked up. And even then she would only stay as long as one of the children held her down. However, if one of the children did something that Skimble didn't like, he would soon let them know with a hiss and a scratch. Dad developed his own special role with the cats. Each night when he came home from work he would whistle. It wasn't long before Peter had learned from his Dad to whistle at every feeding time. Soon the cats would dash from whatever they were doing and follow the whistle, expecting to find food.

Something to think about and do...

What is the best time of the day or week for you?

What is your favourite food/clothes?

Have you got a routine that you prefer?

How do you feel when your routine is changed?

Paint a picture of a journey you make each day or week. Imagine it as a road or river or country path. Instead of mountains, trees etc. add all the routine things you do, as well as the unusual and special events.

School and home

Being on the third floor meant that, at first, the cats stayed in the flat all the time. Then one day, when the children were at school, the door was left open by accident. It was Tabatha who disappeared first, followed reluctantly by Skimble. When Mum realised, she was at her wits' end with worry. She knew that the twins would be terribly upset if anything happened to them. Four o'clock arrived, with the children bursting through the front door as usual. After dropping their bags on the floor and putting their coats on the hanger, Peter went straight to put the cat food out and Alice went to her bedroom, expecting to find Tabatha curled up on her bed. Then Peter realised that Mum had been crying. 'What's wrong, Mum?' he asked. 'I'm so sorry,' she said. 'The cats have gone missing.'

Something to think about and do...

What's the first thing you do when you come home from school?

What helps you to relax?

Have you ever lost anything or have you ever been lost?

Write a poem or story about your first hour back at home after school.

Make a list of the things you would not like to lose and the things that don't matter to you.

Lost and found

Alice came running out of her bedroom when she heard Mum. The three of them hugged each other tightly. 'Will they be all right?' Alice was the first to ask. 'Well, I've phoned Dad and he's coming home early to look for them.'

Peter was quick to suggest he could go out to find them, but Mum was anxious enough without letting Peter outside, especially as it was getting dark.

The children knew Dad was home, as they could hear him whistling outside. They peered through the window, trying to see, but it was all so dark. It seemed ages, but Dad finally walked up the stairs carrying the two kittens. The children, both with tears in their eyes, dashed to the door and rushed at Dad so forcefully that he dropped the two kittens. They scurried into the children's bedroom and hid under the beds.

Something to think about and do...

Have you ever had to wait for anything?

How did you feel?

Have you ever shed tears of sadness and tears of joy?

Draw a person on a piece of paper. On this person colour in the feelings you experience and mark where you feel them. Pick a colour most appropriate for each feeling.

Problems at home

Each night at bedtime, Mum would read a story to the twins in their bedroom. The children had bunk beds, with Peter in the top bunk. Mum would sit on Alice's bed with Peter leaning over to see the pictures. Alice and Peter would often fall asleep before the story was completed and would happily find themselves either dreaming about the ending of the story or about playing with the cats.

Mum would then take the kittens out of the bedroom to the kitchen, where they were expected to stay all night. Tabatha would come happily, but Skimble would bury himself deep under Alice's bed. Mum would struggle to coax him out, sometimes to the sound of Alice begging Mum to leave him in her bedroom. By the time Mum had closed the bedroom door and put the cats to bed, she was both tired and a little annoyed. Dad didn't help by going into the kitchen and accidentally letting the cats out into the lounge. The cats would scratch at the children's bedroom door, asking to be let in. This would often start an argument between Mum and Dad. Sometimes their arguments would be so loud that the children would wake up. Often the children's parents would say sorry to each other, but Peter and Alice wouldn't see or hear this.

Something to think about and do...

What do you do when you go to bed? Read? Watch TV?

What do you like to dream about?

Write down your dreams.

Can you paint or draw your dreams? If you have scary dreams, think about what would make you feel safe. Then add this to your painting.

When you go to sleep, focus on what makes you feel safe.

A difficult night

One night, after a very loud shouting match between their parents, Alice quietly spoke to Peter. 'Are you awake, Pete?' she whispered. 'Yes, what were they arguing about?' asked Peter. 'I think it's about the cats. Do you think they will get rid of them? Mum seems to be so angry about them all the time.' 'I won't let them,' said Peter firmly. Just then they could hear a scratching noise at the door. 'What's that?' asked Alice. Peter didn't wait to answer. He jumped out of bed and quietly opened the door to let Tabatha in. 'Dad must have left the kitchen door open again.' The kitten jumped onto Alice's bed and curled around her legs. Alice stroked the cat. She was pleased to see the kitten but also worried in case Mum came in and was cross. But soon the house was quiet and the children had fallen fast asleep.

The next morning when Mum came into the bedroom to wake the children, she said nothing about Tabatha being in the bedroom. Instead she simply picked up the kitten and took her back to the kitchen. The children didn't say much over breakfast as they were still tired and could see that Mum had been crying.

Something to think about and do...

Do you ever hear noises when you are in bed?

Have you ever heard relatives arguing?

How did you feel?

Do you ever see the relatives making friends after the argument?

Can you tell the people who argue that you sometimes hear them?

Could you ask one of the people who argues whether they ever make up when you are not around?

Draw or paint how you feel when you hear shouting or arguing.

Bad news

A few weeks later, Mum and Dad sat the children down and told them they had something important to share with them. 'You tell them,' said Mum. 'We have something difficult to tell you, children,' Dad said. 'Mum and I have been arguing so much recently that we have decided to live in separate houses. It means we are all going to have to move house. You will both live with Mum, and I will see you at weekends.' After a short silence, Alice said quietly, 'But why can't we just stay here?' 'It's a bit complex to explain,' said Dad. Peter's mind was racing. 'Will we have to change schools?' he asked. 'We're going to move nearer to Grandma and Grandad,' said Mum. 'You'll enjoy that, but it does mean you will have to move to a new school.' Alice began to cry and, as she did so, Tabatha jumped onto her lap. 'What about the cats?' exclaimed Alice. Mum and Dad looked at each other and both sighed. 'We haven't thought about the cats, but we'll work something out about them,' Dad said reluctantly.

The next few weeks all seemed to be a blur for the children and their parents. Peter seemed very cross with his Dad, and Alice spent a lot of her time stroking and caring for the cats.

Something to think about and do...

Have you ever received sad news?

How did you hear and who told you?

How did you react?

What did you feel?

What did you fear?

Can you write a story about your experience?

A long journey

There were a lot of changes in store for the children in the following weeks. Dad found another flat to live in and Mum and the twins moved to a small terraced house near their grandparents. There were some things that the twins enjoyed. It was fun to see more of Grandad and Grandma. It was also new to have stairs to climb in their small house. Alice and Peter now had a bedroom each, which was both positive and negative. Alice missed chatting to Peter late at night when they were supposed to be asleep. Peter said he preferred to have his own bedroom, but he found it strange to be alone at night. The biggest challenge was when the twins went to a new school. They had a new school uniform which felt strange and uncomfortable at first. Peter said very little about his new school, while Alice kept bursting into tears at breakfast time. But their new teachers were really kind, and surprisingly they made new friends quite quickly. Alice joined the music group while Peter was picked to play cricket for the school.

The cats also had to cope with change. They were still not allowed outside because of the busy road. The new house had different rooms to explore, especially when the packing cases were still left around. The cats would climb into the boxes and make themselves all snug and cosy until Mum decided to move the boxes. They would suddenly jump out and dash upstairs to hide under the beds.

Something to think about and do...

What changes have you had to make?

Were they as difficult as you expected?

What do you miss?

Were there any positive things that resulted?

What was the saddest time?

How did you cope with the change?

Think about the changes you have experienced. Make a list of positive things on one side and negative things on the other.

Think of what goes into a first-aid kit (plasters, ointment, thermometer, etc.) Can you draw one?

If you had to make up a first-aid kit that would help you to cope with change, what would it include? (e.g. a special place, a friend to share with, a piece of music to listen to, a book to read, a favourite snack to eat, a diary to write in, a favourite TV show to watch or a computer game to play with.) Make a list or draw a picture to put on your wall to remind you of what helps you at difficult times.

It's all my fault

Life for the twins and the cats had begun to settle into a routine. Each Saturday Dad would come and collect the children to spend the night at his house. Sometimes the twins looked forward to spending the weekend with their Dad. But at other times they preferred to stay at home with their toys and the cats. What they didn't like was the tension that they could feel when Mum knew their Dad was about to knock at the door. It seemed that Mum and Dad did nothing but argue with each other every time they met. Often it was about money or Dad's new girlfriend, but sometimes it was about the twins.

One night, when one of the cats had been sick all over the new lounge carpet and Mum flew into a rage, Alice hid in her bedroom crying. Now that she didn't share her bedroom with her brother, no one knew she was upset. She just lay there thinking that if she hadn't wanted the cats in the first place then Mum and Dad would still be together. 'It was all my fault,' thought Alice, as she cried herself to sleep.

Something to think about and do...

Do you have a routine that you prefer? Make a diary of a typical week that you enjoy.

Do you find yourself spending time at more than one home?

What are the differences?

What do you find your family argue about?

What feelings do you have when it happens?

Have you been blamed for things that were not your fault?

Have you ever blamed yourself for what has happened in your family?

How does this make you feel or react?

Do you ever feel like crying in your bedroom by yourself?

Can you write a letter about how you feel when there are arguments at home? What would you like to say in the letter to your parents?

An emotional outburst

One Saturday, Alice went to ballet class while Peter was playing football for the school team. Dad was supposed to come and watch the match and then pick Alice up from her class. But for one reason or another, Dad was very late. By the time he got to the match, it was almost over. Peter hadn't played brilliantly, so he wasn't in a very good mood. The fact that Dad had almost missed the match didn't help. Dad tried to start a conversation with Peter, who just sat in the car in silence, feeling cross with Dad and himself. By the time they arrived at the ballet class, Alice had been waiting for what seemed ages to her. As Dad got out of the car, Alice burst into tears. 'Where have you been? I thought you'd forgotten me,' she shouted. Dad tried to explain, but no one was listening. Peter exploded with anger, as he tried to protect Alice. 'Look what you've done. It's all your fault. I hate you, I hate you!' he shouted. Dad then got angry with Peter. The journey back to Dad's was made in complete silence.

When the twins got back home to Mum the next day, Alice rushed towards her in tears. Peter said nothing but went straight to his bedroom and played with the cats. Once again, there was tension between Mum and Dad.

Something to think about and do...

How do you behave when you feel cross and angry?

Who do you blame?

Can you be angry with a person and still love them?

How can we tell someone we love them even when we are cross with them?

Make a paper aeroplane and colour it in with the best colours to express your anger. When you feel frustrated and angry, throw the aeroplane as hard as you can.

Do you ever try and protect another person in your family? How do you do this?

What comforts you when you are upset and angry?

A sad farewell

The saddest day was when Mum took Alice and Peter on a car journey with the cats in their cat basket. Mum had arranged to meet another family at a veterinary clinic a short drive away. 'Do we have to let the cats go?' pleaded Alice. 'I'm sorry, children,' Mum said, 'but we just can't cope at home with the cats. I'll be at work each day and you'll be at school. It's just not fair to the cats.' 'Can we have a different pet?' asked Peter sadly. 'Perhaps we could have a guinea pig or some mice?' suggested Alice. 'That sounds more practical,' said Mum.

When they arrived at the clinic, Peter and Alice said 'goodbye' to Tabatha and Skimble. They cuddled them and stroked their coats, and with tears in their eyes, they handed over the cats. No one felt like talking on the journey home. Finally Alice broke the silence. 'Well at least they seemed a nice family. I'm sure they will look after Tabatha and Skimble properly.' 'I think they will be very happy,' said Mum. 'Now they will be living in the countryside and will be able to spend more time outside.'

Something to think about and do...

Have you had to give anything up because of the changes within your family?

What hopes do you have for yourself for the future – in three, five, and ten years' time?

Are there some things you can't change?

What can you change?

Write a short poem about your hopes for the future

A time to adjust

Alice and Peter also found that living just with Mum was very different. Mum seemed more cross, worried and irritable. They would also sometimes hear Mum crying late at night by herself. Going to visit Dad at weekends was also strange. Dad now lived in a very small flat. He also had a new girlfriend called Susan who had a child of her own called Emma. Weekends just didn't seem as relaxing as before for the twins. But some weekends the twins enjoyed themselves, whether with Dad or with Mum.

Alice and Peter never forgot Tabatha and Skimble. At least it looked as if the cats had gone to a good home. Eventually Mum allowed them to have a gerbil each. It wasn't quite the same as having the cats, but it was still good fun.

And what about Tabatha and Skimble? They had no choice but to adjust to a new home and new adventures.

Something to think about and do...

Think about how far you have come since reading this story.

What has changed?

What would you still like to change?

Have you changed your attitude about events, people and yourself?

Treat yourself to something that you enjoy as a reward for completing the book and exercises.

A note to teachers and counsellors

This book can be used as part of a teaching/support/counselling programme with children. Bibliotherapy is a simple way of helping children to relate to their own experiences. By reading each chapter together, the story provides an opportunity for a supporter/counsellor to help the child to draw out their own experiences and thoughts.

The 'Something to think about' sections are tools which you can use practically with a child, using art and writing therapy skills. The book is laid out to allow space for the child to write on the book if they so wish.

Don't try and rush the story; take your time to allow confidence to be built up between you and the child. The story begins by focusing upon issues of self-esteem and confidence-building. It is important to establish these elements before moving on to the more emotional/feeling exercises.

The book may well play just a part of the overall therapy that you offer the child. It is important that the child is able to hold on to various writings/paintings/books etc. so that they can reprocess their thoughts as they continue to grow and develop with age. Children will need to come back to issues time and time again, until they are satisfied with the conclusions they draw and which they then take into adulthood.

If you have any helpful comments after using this book, please visit *www.counsellingcare.org*